Journal Prompts for Self Discovery and Mental Freedom

Storm Keeler

Who are you? What are your goals? *Who do you want to become?*

Goals are not achieved without hard work and dedication. The most overlooked goal in our lives is the goal to be the best version of ourselves we can be. We always want to be better. But, as we know, life gets in the way. In order to be better, we have to know ourselves in-depth. We must acknowledge our weaknesses while leveraging our strengths and setting goals. The question is: *How do I become the person I want to be?* The answer is simple: Work. Explore. Dive deep into yourself. Establish your goals, find your weaknesses, build upon your strengths.

These journal prompts will help you along the way to finding your true self and manifesting the self you wish to be. Write with your heart, think with your soul, and be authentic. This book gives you the start, you write the story. This is your journey to mental freedom and self discovery. Your journal may follow you for a month, this year, years upon years.. No matter what the time-frame is, you're putting in the work. You've made the first step. Now it is your turn to take the wheel.

Be the person you want to be.

Be true to yourself.

Be you.

Who Are You?

1. How do you define yourself at this very moment?

2. Use five words to describe yourself. Write about why you chose each.

____

____

____

____

____

____

____

____

____

____

____

____

____

3. Draw a self portrait. Take note of the areas you emphasized, the areas you neglected, and how all of these details may reflect your self image.

4. If you had unlimited funds to live the life you've always dreamed of, what would that life consist of?

5. What is slowing your progress on these goals? Is anything stopping you from pursuing them?

6. If you were an animal, what animal would you be? Why?

____

____

____

____

____

____

____

____

____

____

____

____

7. What was the most defining moment of your past?

8.   What event in your future are you most looking
     forward to?

9. Where is your safe space? Describe it in detail.

10.   What makes you happiest?

11.   What do you look for in a romantic relationship?
Have your past partners fulfilled your needs?

12.   What is your favorite childhood memory?

13

13. What type of kid were you? Quiet? Angry? Hyper? Sporty?

14.   At what age do you feel you "grew up?"

15.   How do you relax and unwind?

16.   What is your favorite season? Why?

17. Describe what a perfect day would be for you.

18.   What is your love language?

19.   What qualities make you unique?

20. Are you Type A or Type B? How does this affect your life?

21.   What is the nicest thing someone has said to you?

22.   Who is your favorite musician? How have they influenced your life?

23.   What is your favorite book?

24

24.   .How are you feeling today? The past few months? In general?

25. What is spirituality to you? What is sacred in your
    life?

26.   When do you feel most connected to the world?

27.   If you could travel anywhere, where would you go? What would you do?

____

____

____

____

____

____

____

____

____

____

____

____

28. Draw a bridge. One side of the bridge is where you are now. The other side of the bridge is where you want to be. Where are you on the bridge? Is your bridge stable? What sits beneath your bridge? Take note of the details you subconsciously included.

29.   Do you hold yourself in high regard? Why or why not?

30.   What makes you great?

Knowing yourself is an integral part of self improvement. Discovering exactly who you are and where you stand is the foundation of your journey. When you have completed these 30 prompts, read them over, see where you started and if any of your answers have changed. Dedicate time to reflecting on your self discovery portion of your journal

____

____

____

____

____

____

____

____

____

____

What Are Your Goals?

1. Where do you see yourself in five years?

2. Who do you want to be?

37

3. What qualities do you currently lack but want to acquire?

____

____

____

____

____

____

____

____

____

____

____

____

4. How dependent are you? Who do you depend on?

5. Do you enjoy the life you are currently living? Why or why not?

6. Describe your dream life.

7. Draw yourself as a superhero. What superpowers
would you have?

8. What does your dream house look like?

9. Do you want to get married? What does your ideal family consist of?

10.   What are your long-term investments?

11. What is your career path? Are you enjoying your current employment?

12. If you had unlimited finances, what would you invest your money in?

13. What causes do you feel most strongly about?

14. What inspires you?

15. Describe your work ethic.

16. What are your biggest strengths?

17.How can you utilize your strengths to better
your life?

18. Draw a Needs Pyramid.

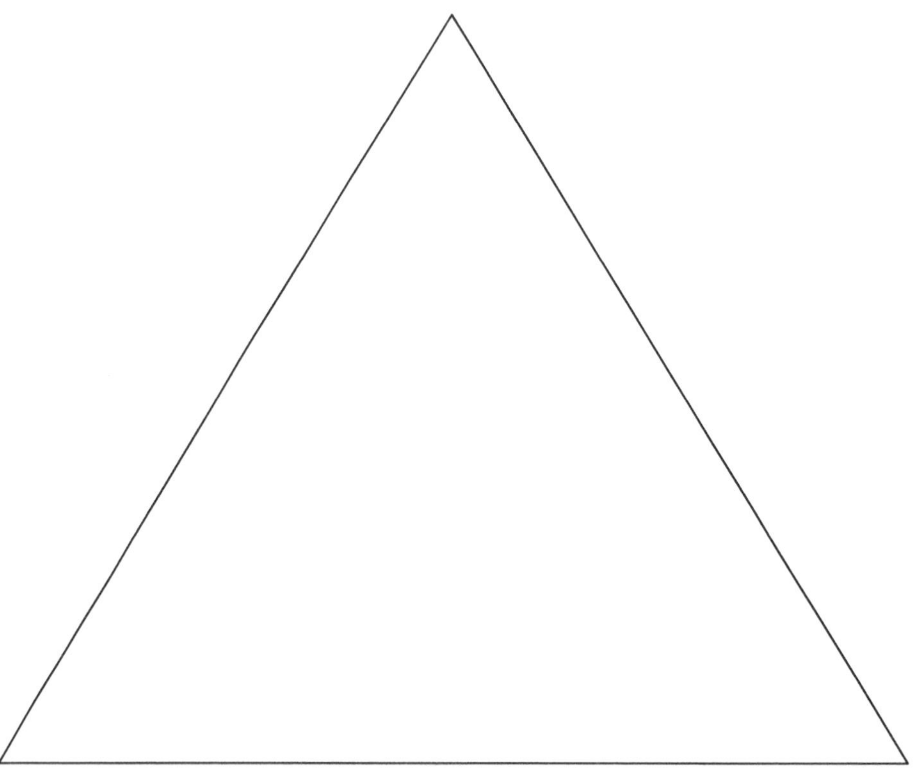

19. Is your physical health where you wish it to be? If not, how can you improve your physical well-being?

20. Are you emotionally stable?

21.Brainstorm ways to improve your financial situation.

22 Who do you admire most? What qualities about
that person do you value?

____

23.Describe your goals. What steps can you take to achieve

them?

____

____

____

____

____

____

____

____

____

____

____

24. What small thing can you start doing today that may impact your future self positively?

25.Brainstorm a five year plan.

Setting goals is an integral part of self improvement. If you want to be better and have a better life, you must know what exactly "better" is to you. Upon completing these 25 prompts, take time to organize your thoughts and plans for how to achieve your goals in all aspects of life.

____

____

____

____

____

____

____

____

____

____

64

Moving Forward

1. How have you grown since starting this journey of self discovery?

2. What have you learned?

3. What changes in your life will you implement in order to achieve your goals?

4. Have you made changes to yourself or behaviors
   since starting this journal?

5. Have you enjoyed journaling?

6. Do you feel you have grown as a person since
   beginning this journey?

____

____

____

____

____

____

____

____

____

____

____

7. What practices will you implement into your life in order to be happier?

8. Write a letter to your past self.

9. Write a letter to your future self.

74

7. Draw a self portrait. Beside it, describe yourself.
   Compare this to your self portrait at the start of this
   journal.

You've achieved something great today. You've completed this journal. You should be proud of yourself for getting this far. Self discovery takes work, and you've put work in.

You've made it this far. Keep pushing forward.

You will achieve your goals.

Believe it.

The last few pages of this journal should be dedicated to reflecting on your journaling experience, how much you've grown, what you've learned, and how you plan on proceeding from here.

Once again, be proud of what you have achieved.

You've taken the first steps towards actualizing your goals.

You have the tools. Forge greatness.

____

____

____

____

____